GUNTHER SCHULLER

FIVE MOODS FOR TUBA QUARTET

Composer's Notes

Taking it to be a basic assumption that a composer in any piece wishes to communicate through the language of music some thoughts, ideas, philosophy, moods, states of mind or emotion, there also can be from time to time subsidiary purposes which also motivate a composition. In the case of *Five Moods*, one crucial factor was the passing of William Bell, the first great American artist on the tuba and the mentor and teacher of many of today's finest tubists. Indeed, *Five Moods*, dedicated to Mr. Bell's memory, tries to capture in vignette portraits the different characteristic traits of this remarkable man.

In addition, as a composer who also is a brass player, I always welcome the opportunity to write challenging, serious music for these instruments and particularly for the tuba which has for so many years suffered from stereotyping at the hands of composers and has generally been considered an "underdog" instrument, not regarded as capable of a full range of musical expression. But it is precisely Bill Bell's artistry and teaching which gave that particular myth the lie. In a real sense, his legacy is the wealth of literature the tuba can now boast and the inspiration he has given to men like Harvey Phillips, who suggested that I write this piece for the first International Tuba Symposium-Workshop (held in Bloomington, Indiana) and who carries on in Mr. Bell's tradition.

G.S.

Associated Music Publishers, Inc.

DISTRIBUTED BY

HAL•LEONARD® CORPORATION

7777 W. BLUEMOUND RD. P.O. BOX 13819 MILWAUKEE, WI 53213

Commissioned by Harvey Phillips
in memory of William Bell

Five Moods
for Tuba Quartet

GUNTHER SCHULLER

1. Lament

poco rit.
a tempo
10
p
f
5
5
5
5
espr.
5
mp
dim.
pp
mp
dim.
pp
mp
dim.
pp
mp
dim.
pp
15
mfp < f
mp
flzg.
f
p < mf
5
f
mfp
f
mp
f
mfp
f
mp

espr.
dim.
mp
espr.
dim.
mp
espr.
dim.
mp
espr.
dim.
mp
f
dim. poco a poco
f
dim. poco a poco
f molto legato
3
dim. poco a poco
f molto legato
dim. poco a poco
20
rit. al fine
lunga
p
dim.
lunga
ppp
p
dim.
lunga
ppp
p
dim.
ppp
lunga
p
p
p
pp

2.

Allegro moderato ♩ = 72–80
Un poco giocoso
con sord.
con sord.
con sord.
con sord.
mp
p
p
con sord.
mp
p
pp
con sord.
mp
pp
p
pp
tr
tr
mf
mf
f
pp sub.
mf
p
f sub.
f
mf
pp sub.
p
f sub.
mf
f
mf
p
f sub.
tr
pp sub.
p
f sub.
pp
mf
f
pp
mf
f
pp
mf
f
pp
mf
f
5
10

25
30
sfz
mf
p
pp
sfz
mf
p
pp
sfz
mf
p
pp
sfz
mf
p
pp
p
p
p
p
5
5
pp
mp
pp
mp
pp
mp
pp
mp

3.

(a) Diamond-shaped notes indicate singing or humming.
(b) With apologies to Igor.

Five Moods
for Tuba Quartet

2nd Tuba

GUNTHER SCHULLER

1. Lament

2nd Tuba

2nd Tuba
10 ♩= 90
p
mf marc.
5
15
mp
3
3
3
f sub.
3
mp leggiero
5
20
p
2
f
3 3 3 3
3
pp
25
♩ = ♩. (without attack on initial notes)
pp
30
(pp)
35
cresc.
f
G.P.
2
with finality
mf
f
May 24, 1973

2nd Tuba

4.
Molto lento, broodingly ♩ = ca. 40
mf
p
pp
5
pp < p
mp
pp
molto legato
5
5
5
cresc. poco a poco
movendo
7
mp
10 definite attack
5
mp
mf (smooth legato)
p
mf
Tempo I, tranquillo
lunga possibile
3
f tenuto
pp
senza dim.
attacca
5.
Allegro volando (in 2)
♩. = ca. 90
mf
f
p
5
pp legg.
mp
mp
p
(♩. = ♩)
p

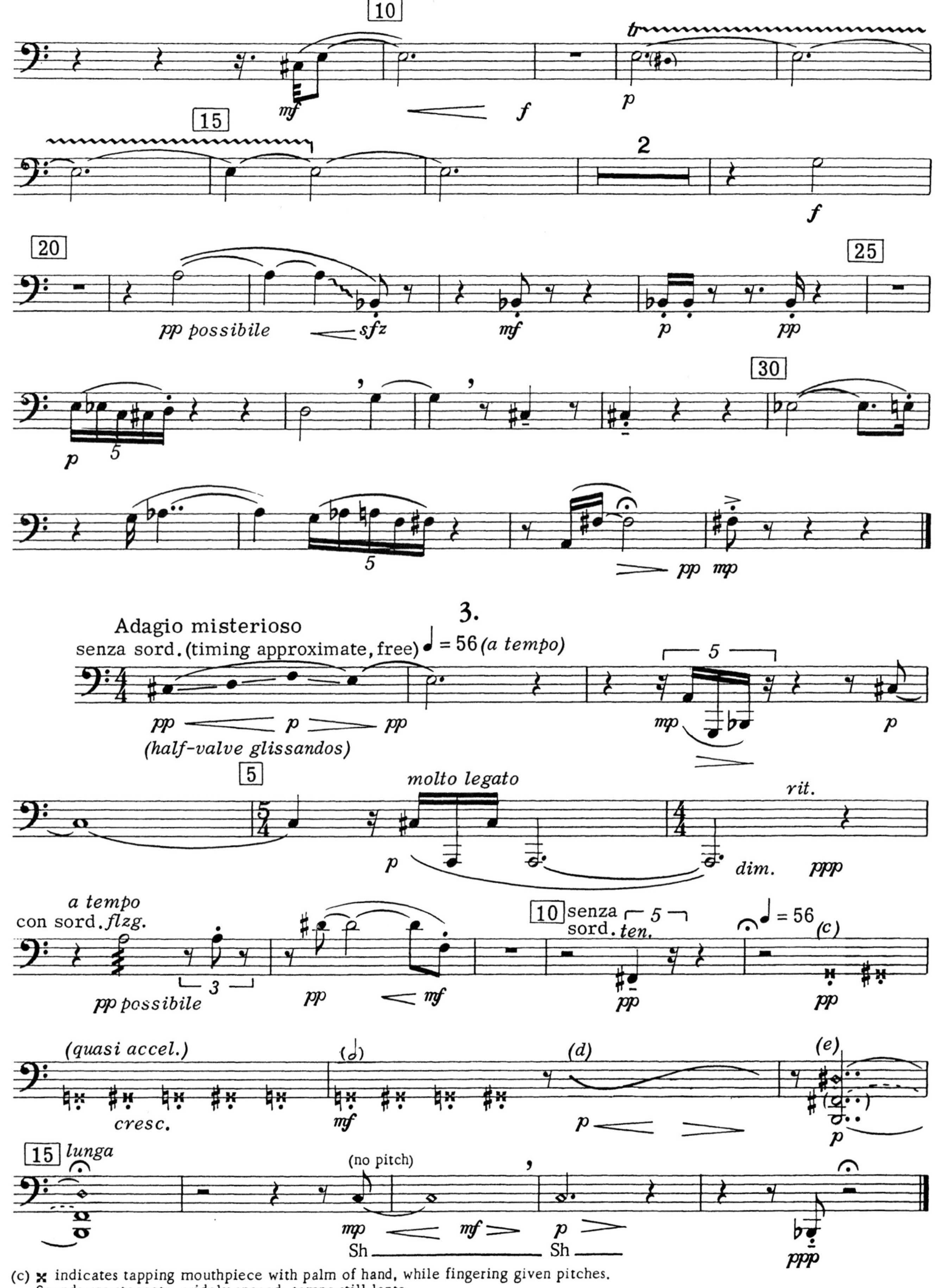

(c) ✕ indicates tapping mouthpiece with palm of hand, while fingering given pitches.
Sounds are staccato, widely spaced; tempo still lento.
(d) Blow air into instrument without producing pitch, producing low whistling or swishing sound.
(e) Each player sustains until end of breath. Releases are not coordinated. (Middle notes in triads are sympathetic vibrations.)

Commissioned by Harvey Phillips
in memory of William Bell

Five Moods
for Tuba Quartet

3rd Tuba

GUNTHER SCHULLER

1. Lament

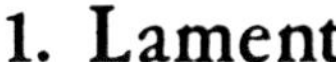

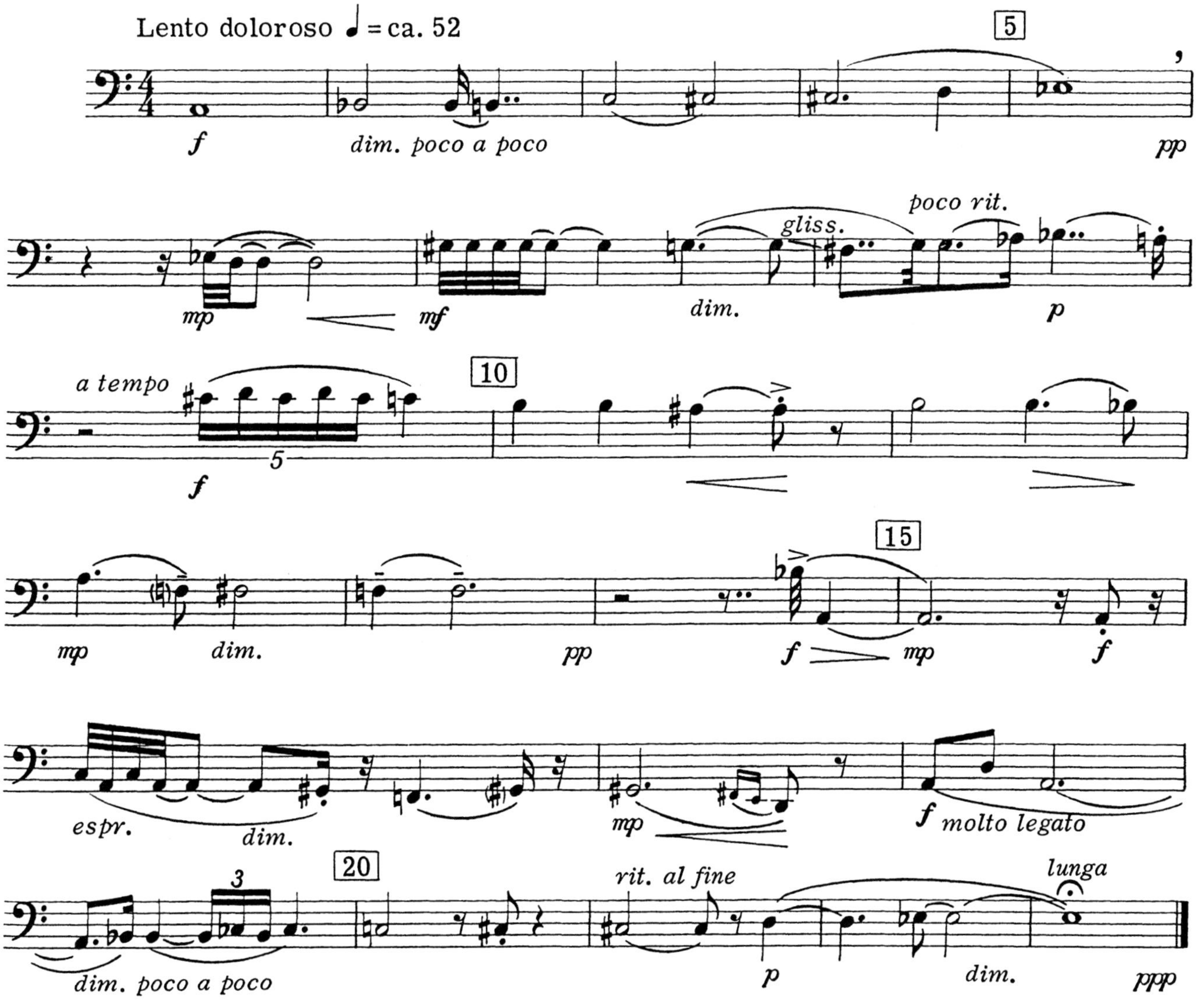

2.

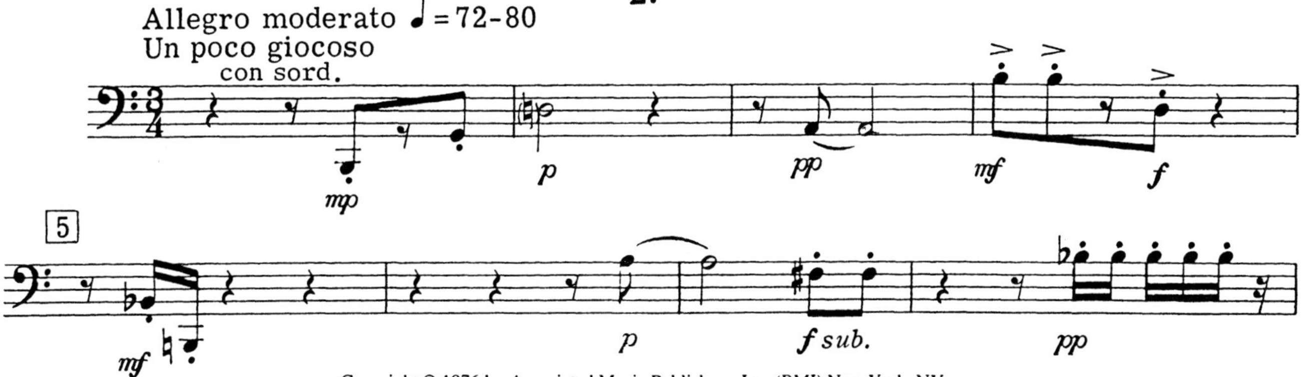

10   ♩ = 90
5
3
15
p
mf marc.
mp
secco
p   3   3
20
p
f   3   3   3   3
25   flzg.
pp
3
f   pp
mf
30
p   mf
35
mp   cresc.
G.P.   with finality
2
stacc.   f   mf   f
May 24, 1973

4.

Molto lento, broodingly ♩ = ca. 40

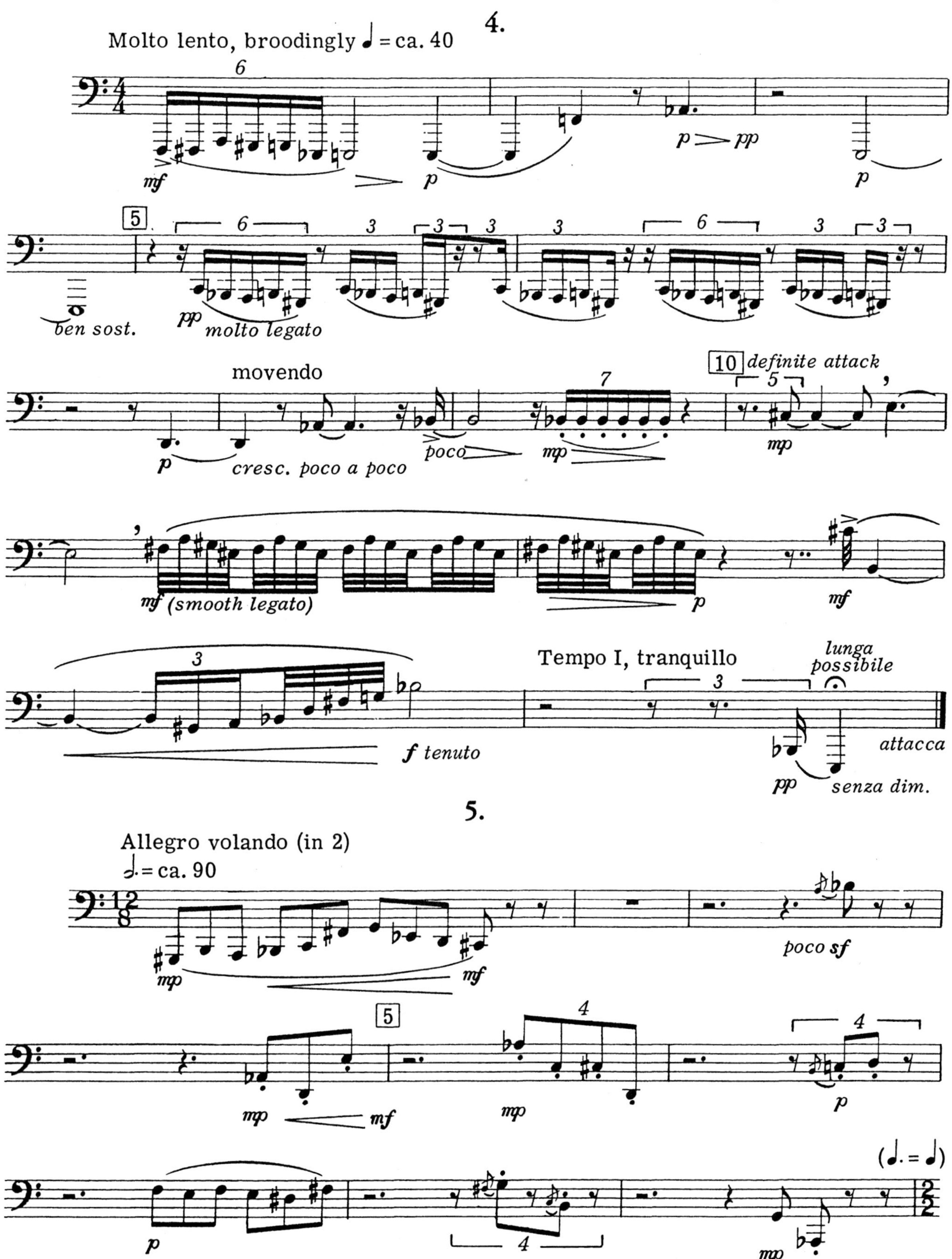

5.

Allegro volando (in 2)
♩. = ca. 90

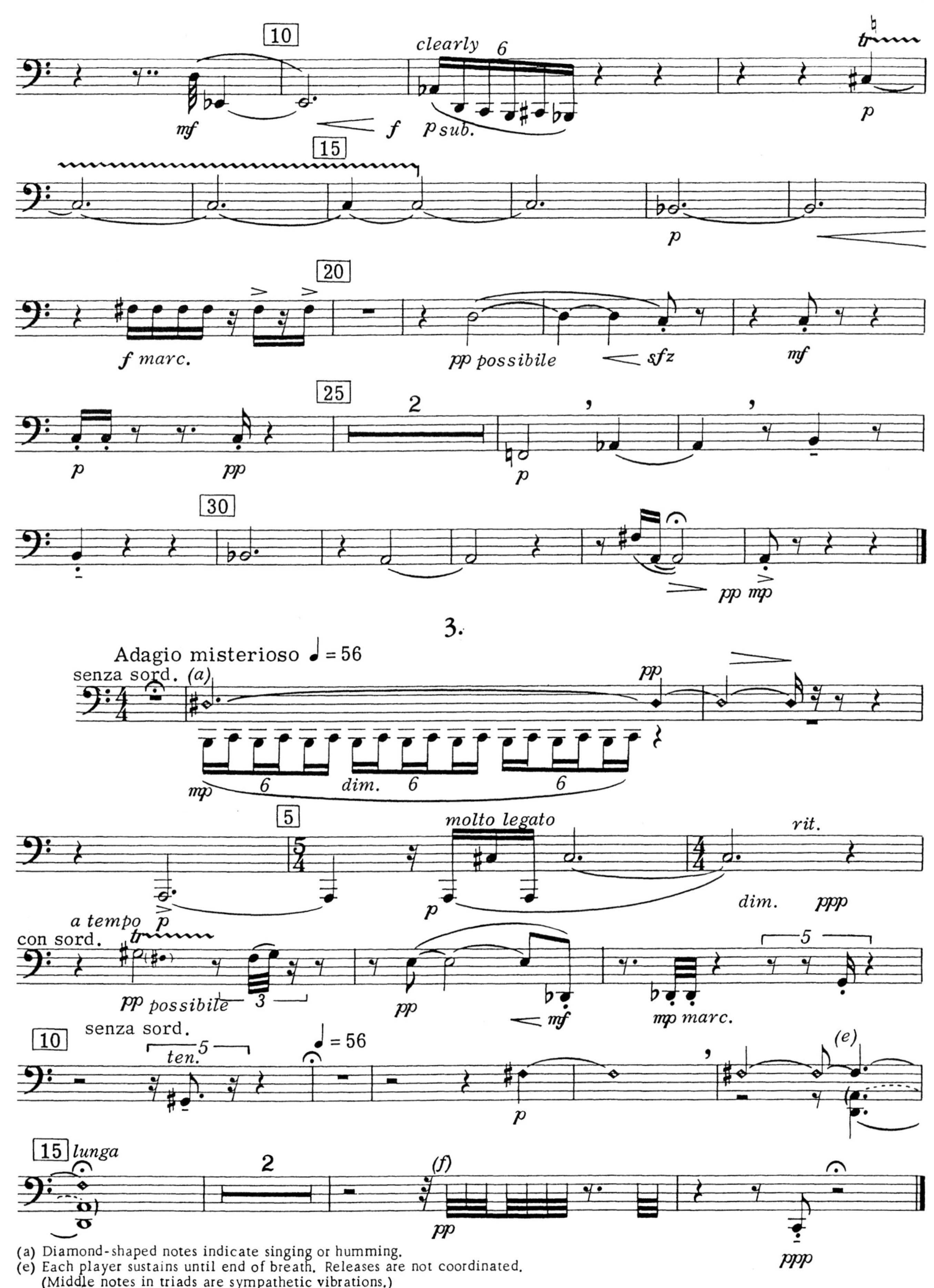

(a) Diamond-shaped notes indicate singing or humming.
(e) Each player sustains until end of breath. Releases are not coordinated.
    (Middle notes in triads are sympathetic vibrations.)
(f) With small triangle stick, tap edge or side of bell.

Five Moods
for Tuba Quartet

1. Lament

4th Tuba

3.

(b) With apologies to Igor.
(d) Blow air into instrument without producing pitch, producing low whistling or swishing sound.
(e) Each player sustains until end of breath. Releases are not coordinated.
    (Middle notes in triads are sympathetic vibrations.)

2.
Allegro moderato ♩ = 72-80
Un poco giocoso
con sord.
p
pp
mf
f
pp sub.
p
f sub.
pp
mf
f
mp
p
p
p
f marc.
f
pp possibile
sfz
mf
p
pp
p
p
30
pp mp

(c) ✕ indicates tapping mouthpiece with palm of hand, while fingering given pitches.
     Sounds are staccato, widely spaced; tempo still lento.
(d) Blow air into instrument without producing pitch, producing low whistling or swishing sound.
(e) Each player sustains until end of breath. Releases are not coordinated. (Middle notes in triads are sympathetic vibrations.)
(f) With small triangle stick, tap edge or side of bell.

4.

Molto lento, broodingly ♩ = ca. 40
a little brusquely
(slow trill)
molto legato
ben sost.
molto legato
(slow trill)
mp sub.

movendo
definite attacks
10
cresc. poco a poco
mp
espr. sost.
cresc. poco a poco
mp
cresc. poco a poco
poco
mp
cresc. poco a poco
mp
mf (smooth legato)
mf (smooth legato)
p
mf
mf (smooth legato)
p
mf
mf (smooth legato)
p
mf
Tempo I, tranquillo
lunga possibile
f tenuto
pp
senza dim.
f tenuto
pp
senza dim.
f tenuto
pp
senza dim.
attacc
f tenuto
pp
senza dim.
f tenuto
pp
senza dim.

5.

Allegro volando (in 2) ♩. = ca. 90
p sub.
mf
f
mf
f
mp
mf
mp
f
poco sf
p
mp
mp
mp
mf
p
5
p sub.
pp
pp
pp legg.
mp
4
p
mp
2
p

10 (♩=90)
♩. = ♩
p sub.
p
secco
ten.
mp
mf
mf marc.
mp

f sub.
p
3
3
f
20
mp
leggiero
5
p
p
b
p
12
8
sub. mf
p
f
3
3
3
3
pp
f
3
3
3
3
pp
f
3
3
3
3
pp
f
pp

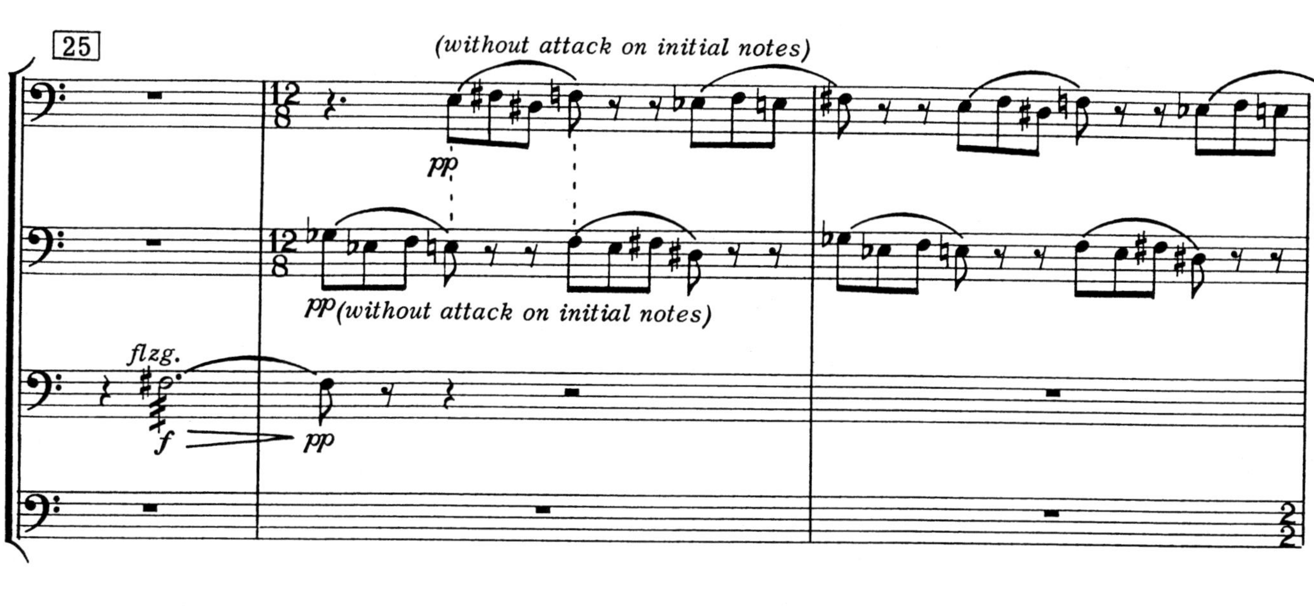
25
(without attack on initial notes)
pp
pp (without attack on initial notes)
flzg.
f
pp

mf
mf

30
3
p
mf
mf
mf

(pp)
(pp)
mp
mp
mf
stacc.
35
cresc.
cresc.
cresc.
stacc.
cresc.
f
f
f
f
G.P.
2
with finality
mf
mf
mf
mf
mf
f
f
f
f
f
May 24, 1973

Five Moods
for Tuba Quartet

1st Tuba

GUNTHER SCHULLER

1. Lament

1st Tuba

10 ♩ = 90
p
mf
p sub.
p
15
20
25 ♩ = ♩.
f
pp
pp (without attack on initial notes)
30
(pp)
35
cresc.
f
G.P.
with finality
mf
f
May 24, 1973

1st Tuba

4.

Molto lento, broodingly ♩ = ca. 40
a little brusquely
mf
p pp
mf p
(slow trill)
tr
pp
poco
p pp
p pp
movendo
tr
p
cresc. poco a poco
mp
7
definite attack
5
mp
espr. sost.
mf (smooth legato)
Tempo I, tranquillo
lunga possibile
f tenuto
pp
attacca
senza dim.

5.

Allegro volando (in 2)
♩. = ca. 90
mf f
p sub.
p mf
p sub.
pp
pp
p mf
(♩. = ♩)
p pp

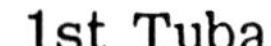

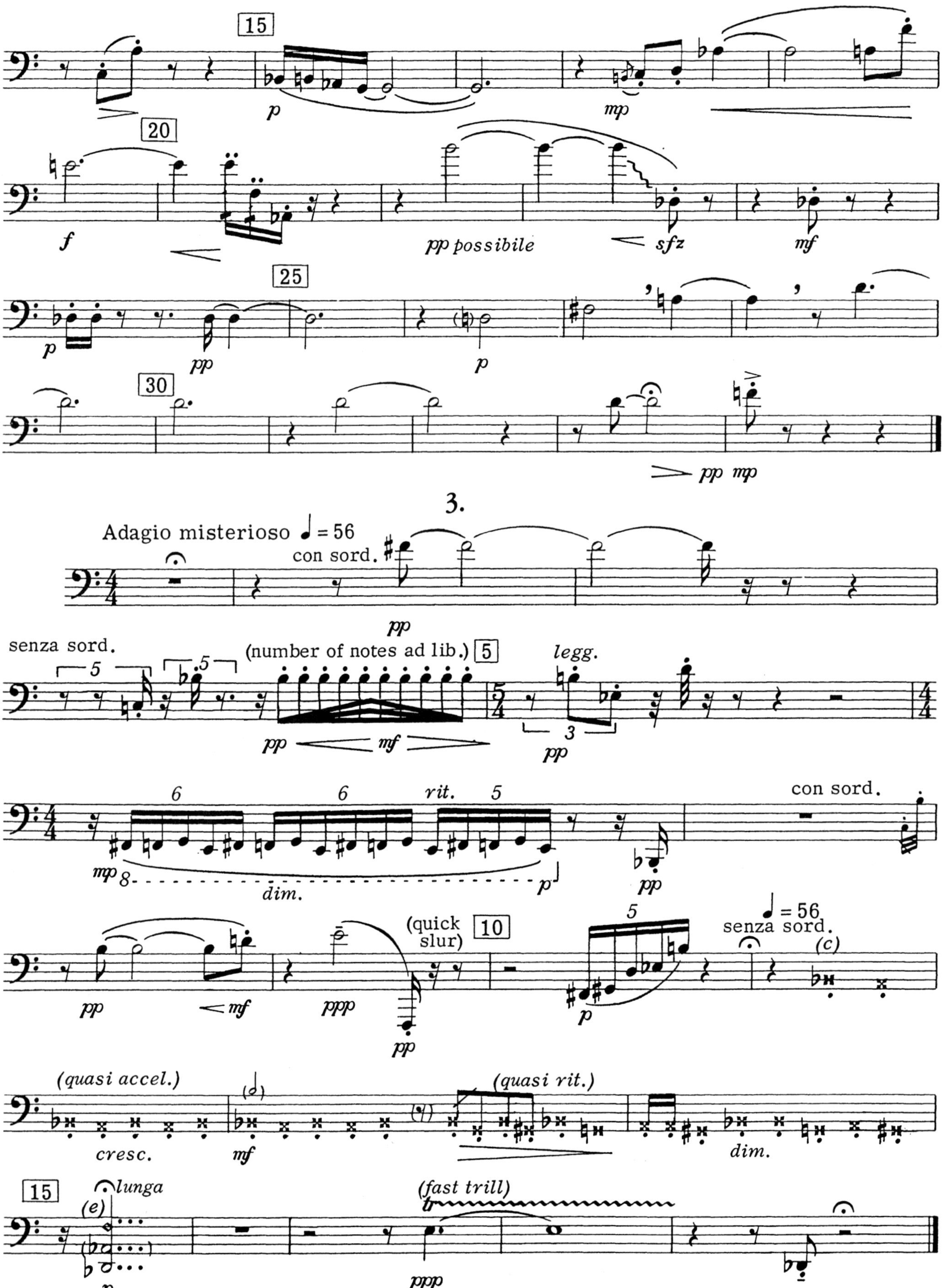

(c) ✕ indicates tapping mouthpiece with palm of hand, while fingering given pitches.
Sounds are staccato, widely spaced; tempo still lento.
(e) Each player sustains until end of breath. Releases are not coordinated. (Middle notes in triads are sympathetic vibrations.)